Passport2Purity

Tour Guide
Parent's Manual

hosted by

Dennis & Barbara
RAINEY

FamilyLife Publishing®
Little Rock, Arkansas

Published by FamilyLife, a ministry of Campus Crusade for Christ.
First edition 1999. Second edition 2004.

Printed in the United States of America.
ISBN: 978-1-57229-656-5
12 11 10 09 08 3 4 5 6 7 8

Illustrations by Steve Björkman.

Dennis Rainey, President
5800 Ranch Drive
Little Rock, AR 72223
1-800-FL-TODAY
www.familylife.com

A ministry of Campus Crusade for Christ

Tour Guide
Parent's Manual

TABLE OF CONTENTS

SECTION TWO: ADVENTURE JOURNAL

WHAT IS PASSPORT2PURITY®?

Key Objectives

- ★ Connect your heart to your son or daughter before he or she enters the teen years.
- ★ Create a heart-to-heart time for some of life's most intimate issues.
- ★ Help your child decide in advance what his convictions will be, based on God's Word.

Preparation

(1-2 weeks)

★ Pray ★ Review Passport2Purity ★ Plan getaway
★ Invite preteen ★ Gather your materials ★ Pack

Kickoff

(Friday—5 p.m.)

★ Dinner together ★ Explain purpose
★ Present *Adventure Journal* ★ Read letters

Getaway

(Friday—6:30 p.m.)

★ Session One: "Blastoff" in car ★ Arrive at destination and settle in
★ Finish Session One ★ Session Two: "Running With the Herd"

(Saturday—8:30 a.m.)

★ Breakfast ★ Session Three: "Growing to Sexual Maturity"
★ Session Four: "Staying Pure"

(Saturday—afternoon)

★ Lunch ★ Fun time ★ Clean up for dinner

(Saturday—6 p.m.)

★ Session Five: "It's a Date!"

Celebration Dinner

★ Nice dinner ★ Present My Passport ★ Give gift
★ Encourage and pray a blessing on your preteen

PREPARATION CHECKLIST FOR BUSY PARENTS

This checklist will help you organize, but please review all the chapters in the Tour Guide so you are well-prepared for a successful getaway with your son or daughter.

To Do

(Refer to Chapters One, Two, and Three)

- ❏ Review Passport2Purity audio and written material.
- ❏ Complete "How Well Do You Know Your Preteen" (Chapter Six).
- ❏ Schedule time off work (if required).
- ❏ Determine your budget.
- ❏ Choose dates and destination.
- ❏ Dinner reservations (if required).
- ❏ Lodging, car, and travel reservations.
- ❏ Plan your fun activity.
- ❏ Obtain tickets (if required).
- ❏ Invite your preteen.
- ❏ Write letters in his journal.
- ❏ Purchase a special gift (optional).
- ❏ Review your convictions and discuss them with your spouse (Chapter Five).
- ❏ Read preparation for the sex talk (if needed).
- ❏ Glue a recent photo of your child in his journal.
- ❏ Glue four photos of yourself in his journal.
- ❏ Arrange care for other children, pets, and your home.
- ❏ Pack early.
- ❏ Pray a lot!

To Take

- ❏ Passport2Purity.
- ❏ Bible (one for each of you).
- ❏ Camera and film (or camcorder).
- ❏ Money for meals and fun activity.
- ❏ CD player for use in car and getaway location.
- ❏ Batteries for CD player (if needed).
- ❏ Pens or pencils (sharpened).
- ❏ Appropriate clothing for fun activity.
- ❏ Appropriate clothing for celebration dinner.
- ❏ Special gear needed for fun activity.
- ❏ Snacks.

Project Supplies to Gather

(Refer to Chapter Four)

- ❑ One gallon of water for projects (if not readily available at your destination).
- ❑ Easy 100-piece jigsaw puzzle.
- ❑ Difficult 100-piece jigsaw puzzle.
- ❑ Timer.
- ❑ Small prize for puzzle contest.
- ❑ Small sack for puzzle pieces.
- ❑ Five paper grocery bags to hold projects.
- ❑ Clear two-quart pitcher with removable top.
- ❑ Six clear plastic cups.
- ❑ Three different types of "pollution."
- ❑ Plastic bags to hold pollution ingredients.
- ❑ Long-handle spoon.
- ❑ One-gallon plastic bag.
- ❑ Box of wooden safety matches.
- ❑ A few helium-grade, latex balloons.
- ❑ Thin, sharp needle (thread with colorful string).
- ❑ Roll of transparent tape.
- ❑ Six sheets of construction paper (three red, three yellow).
- ❑ White school glue.

Passport2Purity®

Section One
Planning Your Getaway

Content Advisory

As you review the Passport2Purity materials, you'll soon realize that we are addressing some truly significant topics. You will be connecting heart-to-heart on some of life's most intimate issues. We believe most pivotal life choices are made between the ages of eleven and fifteen. You must be proactive to help your preteen decide in advance about the traps of adolescence ... or the culture will. Go for it!

Special Note

To enhance readability, when referring to your preteen, we have chosen to use male pronouns throughout most of this material. The English language does not provide a simple, gender-neutral pronoun to reference a boy or a girl.

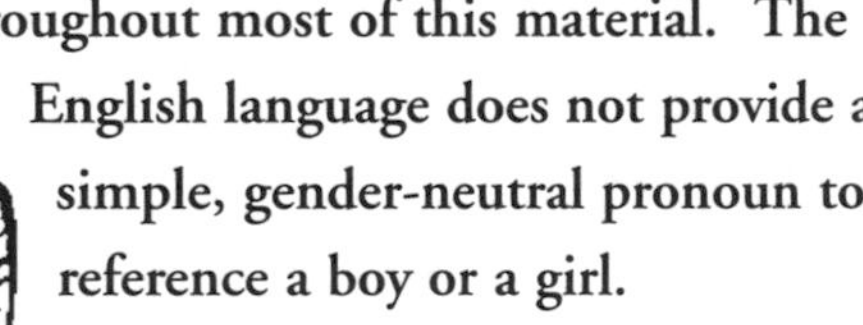

CHAPTER ONE

THE Passport2Purity GETAWAY

CONTENTS

In addition to the Tour Guide for parents, this package includes the following components:

- "Nine Steps to a Successful Getaway," an encouraging, instructional audio message for parents

- Five CDs containing five messages by Dennis and Barbara Rainey:

Session One:	"Blastoff"—orientation to Passport2Purity; authority of God's Word
Session Two:	"Running With the Herd"—handling peer pressure; good friends
Session Three for Daughters:	"Growing to Sexual Maturity"—physical changes and "the talk" for girls (with Barbara Rainey)
Session Three for Sons:	"Growing to Sexual Maturity"—physical changes and "the talk" for boys (with Dennis Rainey)
Session Four:	"Staying Pure"—developing moral courage when facing sexual temptation
Session Five:	"It's a Date"—straight talk about dating and its purpose

- *Adventure Journal*—a note-taking guide for your preteen

- My Passport—a special document to present to your preteen that commemorates your getaway experience

- Five Adventure Stamps to place at the end of each session of your preteen's *Adventure Journal*, plus one Adventure Stamp for My Passport

GETAWAY SCHEDULE

We are providing a sample schedule to follow for planning purposes. For simplicity, we have chosen Friday night through Saturday evening. You may want to modify this schedule and allow some flexibility to fit your family's needs, but it is very important that you maintain your focus on your preteen. Your attention, as well as your inattention, will speak volumes to your child about the value you have placed on this event.

FRIDAY EVENING

1. Go to dinner at a place your preteen likes and where he feels comfortable. (Try to leave early in the afternoon, especially if you have a long drive.)

   - At some point during dinner, explain the purpose of the weekend: to have fun together and to talk about some important issues that your preteen will soon face.

   - Give your preteen his *Adventure Journal.*

   - Ask him to open it and read the letters from you and your spouse. (See pages F and G in Section Two of this book for writing instructions.)

2. Drive to your final destination.

   - During the drive begin playing Session One, "Blastoff," in the car. This includes an orientation for your getaway plus two Scripture memory songs: Colossians 1:18 and Psalm 119:105.

   - Instruct your preteen to fill in the note-taking outline in his *Adventure Journal* as you drive.

3. Stop the message when Dennis indicates it's time to do the first project.

4. Arrive at location. Unpack and settle in.

5. Finish Session One in the *Adventure Journal.*

   - Complete the project "Puzzled."

   - Return to the audio message. After Dennis announces the next session and you hear the memory verse song, stop the CD.

   - Complete the Icebreaker discussion questions (Refer to page 6.)

   - Mark the completion of this material by placing one of the six Adventure Stamps on the printed image of the seal at the end of Session One in your child's *Adventure Journal.* Remember to sign and date the page.

   Allow one hour and 10 minutes for this session, excluding dinner, traveling, and settling in.

6. Take a 15-minute break.

7. Complete Session Two: "Running With the Herd."
   This will consist of:

   - An audio message by Dennis Rainey

   - A Scripture memory song: 1 Corinthians 15:33-34a

   - The project "Dirty Water"

- "Make Up Your Mind" discussion questions (Refer to page 13.)

- Adventure Stamp

Allow one hour and 20 minutes for this session, but be flexible with your time and talk as long as you want.

SATURDAY MORNING

NOTE: Start early enough to stay on schedule and complete your plans.

1. Eat breakfast. Be ready to start the next session by 8:30 a.m.

2. Complete Session Three: "Growing to Sexual Maturity." This will consist of:

   - An audio message by Barbara Rainey (for daughters) or Dennis Rainey (for sons)

   - A Scripture memory song: 1 Corinthians 6:18-20

   - The project "Burned Up"

   - "Make Up Your Mind" discussion questions (Refer to page 22 for girls or page 30 for boys.)

   - Adventure Stamp

   Allow one hour and 35 minutes for this session.

IMPORTANT NOTE: *A short exhortation on the subject of masturbation is provided on the CD after Session Three. Unique messages are given to boys and girls. Review this before your getaway to be sure you are comfortable with it. While some child development experts take a different view, we believe our perspective is the biblical standard. There is a break on the CD after Session Three. If you decide you don't want your child to hear this message now, stop the CD and move directly to the project. Otherwise, listen to the brief masturbation message. If you choose not to use this message, be sure to discuss this topic in your own way.*

3. Take a 15-minute break.

4. Complete Session Four, "Staying Pure." This will consist of:

   - An audio message by Dennis Rainey
   - A Scripture memory song: Song of Solomon 8:4 (NIV)
   - The project "Leaky Balloon"
   - "Make Up Your Mind" discussion questions (Refer to page 36.)
   - Adventure Stamp

   Allow one hour and 45 minutes for this session.

SATURDAY AFTERNOON

1. Eat lunch.

2. FREE TIME: **Do something fun together!**

Make this fun time a **BIG DEAL!** This is an incredible opportunity for connecting with your preteen and making the entire getaway memorable.

See Chapter Three for instructions and a list of potential ideas.

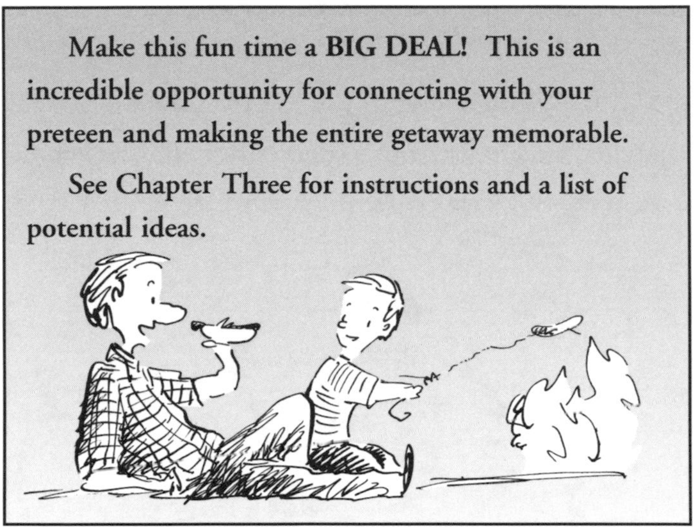

SATURDAY EVENING

1. Rest, get cleaned up, and get dressed for dinner. Start your last session by 6 p.m.

2. Complete Session Five, "It's a Date!" This will consist of:

   - An audio message by Dennis Rainey
   - A Scripture memory song: Philippians 2:3-4
   - The project "Glued Up"
   - "Make Up Your Mind" discussion questions (Refer to page 44.)

- The Wait-to-Date Contract
- Adventure Stamp

Allow one hour and 30 minutes for this session.

NOTE: Don't skip Session Five! If you had to take more time on earlier sessions and time ran out, be sure to come back to this on another day. Schedule the time with your preteen right now.

3. Have a celebration dinner at a nice restaurant, and wrap up your weekend getaway with a small ceremony.

    - Present your preteen with the My Passport document. In his presence, place the final Adventure Stamp inside, then sign and date the document.
    - If you purchased a special gift for your child, give it to him now (see suggestions in Chapter Three).
    - Encourage him that he has entered an exciting new phase. Let him know that you're going to view him in a new light—as a little more grown up and "clued in" on some adult things.

- KEY: **During your celebration dinner (or in the car before you drive home), take your child by the hand and bless him. Ask the Lord to guide him, protect him from the evil one, keep him from temptation, and help him grow to become God's man (or woman) as he moves through adolescence into adulthood.**

4. On your way home, listen to Dennis Rainey's closing comments on CD 4, Track 4.

AFTER YOUR GETAWAY

1. Determine some follow-up times to complete the "Going the Extra Mile" studies in the back of the *Adventure Journal.* Ask your child to go over one study at a time, and then get together to discuss it.

2. Keep praying with and for your child.

3. Stay connected! Continue to pursue your relationship with your son or daughter and pass on spiritual insights.

4. We stongly recommend that you find a good ongoing discipleship program to work through together over the next year or so.

CHAPTER TWO

ARE YOU READY FOR AN ADVENTURE?

A Special Word from Dennis Rainey

Passport2Purity will provide the tools and encouragement you need to create a special getaway to talk about critical issues your preteen will face in the years ahead.

A friend of mine told me a story about his teenage son who was teased unmercifully by his buddies because he was a virgin. "When are you going to become a real man?" they taunted.

Finally this young man replied, "You know, I could become just like you anytime I want to. I could have sex. But you can never again become like me. You can never become a virgin again."

This was a teenager who was living by his convictions. He had decided in advance that he was going to abstain from sexual immorality. He was going to protect his innocence until he was married. He wanted God's best for his life and his marriage, and he didn't care what type of pressure he felt from his friends.

Those are the types of convictions my wife, Barbara, and I have been building into our own six children. Our prayer is that you have the same desire. And our hope is that Passport2Purity will provide the tools and encouragement you need to create a special getaway to discuss critical issues your preteen will face in the coming years. This could be one of the best investments you will make in the life of your preteen.

This product is designed for a mother and daughter or a father and son when the child is aged ten to fifteen. To me, however, the best time to plan your getaway would be before your preteen turns thirteen. Barbara took each of our preteen girls (and I took each of our preteen boys) on a weekend getaway like this because we've found that the preteen years are when children are most teachable, more open, and less independent.

Your Passport2Purity weekend will include audio messages, creative audio dramas, music, discussion times, and special projects. And, of course, you will want to schedule some activities that will be just plain fun. This planning workbook will take you step by step through the planning process for your getaway (see Chapter Three).

A WINDOW OF OPPORTUNITY

My guess is that 99.9 percent of all parents look at their eleven- or twelve-year-old and don't have the foggiest idea that he is beginning to grapple with adult issues. Preadolescents don't know how to connect all the dots—for example, they may only understand the basic facts about sex. But their own sex drive is emerging, and they are sensing a new, often frightening need to be accepted and appreciated by the opposite sex. Life is in full gear. Determinative life choices are about to be made.

This is no time for parents to curl up on the couch for a nap. Instead, there is a twelve- to twenty-four-month window of opportunity in the fifth- and sixth-grade years to prepare the preteen for the turmoil of junior high. Our experience leads us to believe the most pivotal choices are made during

This is no time for parents to curl up on the couch for a nap.

the age span of about eleven to fifteen. Wrong choices can tragically alter the course of a child's life. During your getaway, you will be connecting heart-to-heart on some of life's most intimate issues. You must be proactive to train and prepare your preteen for adolescence ... or the culture will do it for you. By taking your preteen on a Passport2Purity getaway, you are taking a very proactive step. I commend you for your love for your child and for your courage!

THE TRAPS OF ADOLESCENCE

Just think of when you were navigating the teenage years. Do you remember some of the difficult issues you had to face? Imagine that your children have been walking along a path through meadows and fields. At thirteen, the path leads them into a dense, brooding forest. They know that on the other side of the forest is the city where they will spend their adult years. But in order to make it to adulthood, they must walk through the forest barefoot and blindfolded. Hidden in that forest are traps designed to capture, injure, maim, or even kill them.

Kids face a trap today that didn't even exist for us as parents. Many teens are unwittingly lured into adult Internet chat rooms and ensnared in sexual activity. For some it leads to only one place ... DEATH! Internet stalking is for real ... BELIEVE IT!

As a parent, you know where the traps are hidden because you've already been through the forest. You know how vulnerable and naïve a young teenager is; perhaps you were caught by some of these traps yourself, and you know how dangerous they are. It's your job to guide your children through to the other side. You can't pick them up and carry them to adulthood. They have to walk the path. But they need you as their guide.

Although they seldom admit it, deep down, most teens desperately want their mom and dad to come beside them and say, "You know, there are some things that I wish I had told you earlier, but I didn't, so I want to tell you now. I want to be a part of your life as you go through these teenage years. I want to be there for you. I want to help you avoid the traps of adolescence."

Passport2Purity is designed to help you begin preparing your preteen for several of these traps: peer pressure, sex, and dating. Barbara and I cover these traps, as well as many others, in greater detail in our book *Parenting Today's Adolescent*, published by Thomas Nelson, Inc., Publishers. We encourage you to read a copy as you work through the planning process for this weekend. Passport2Purity is designed to build upon the concepts discussed in this book.

CHALLENGE TO THE HIGHEST STANDARD

If you were asked, "What are you teaching your child about sex and morality?" my guess is that you might say something like, "We are teaching him that he should wait until he is married to begin having sex."

The leadership at FamilyLife has developed a strong conviction that virginity is not a high enough goal.

How do you think your teenager will interpret and apply "wait until marriage before having sex"? Would he answer "being a virgin on my wedding night" or "everything but intercourse" or … what?

In this culture, challenging your child with the goal of virginity is excellent. But the leadership at

FamilyLife has developed a strong conviction that virginity is not a high enough goal. Nor is it the ultimate biblical goal. Unfortunately, studies have found that even our Christian teenagers are engaging in sexual activities reserved for marriage, yet they are maintaining "technical virginity."

This point was underscored during a recent television news report on churches that are teaching abstinence to their teens. One teenage girl who was interviewed was adamant about maintaining her virginity until she was married. Yet, in the next breath she mentioned that heavy kissing and petting were okay as long as she didn't engage in sexual intercourse!

Scripture does not command us to preserve a "technical virginity." The Bible presents a number of pointed principles to ensure that our relationships with the opposite sex are appropriate and rewarding. The key words underlying all of them are purity and holiness. Here are several basic passages:

For this is the will of God, your sanctification; that is, that you abstain from sexual immorality; that each of you know how to possess his own vessel in sanctification and honor, not in lustful passion, like the Gentiles who do not know God. ... For God has not called us for the purpose of impurity, but in sanctification.

—1 Thessalonians 4:3-5, 7

Flee immorality. Every other sin that a man commits is outside the body, but the immoral man sins against his own body. Or do you not know that your body is a temple of the Holy Spirit who is in you, whom you have from God, and that you are not your own? For you have been bought with a price: therefore glorify God in your body.

—1 Corinthians 6:18-20

The goal of our instruction with our children is ... helping our children protect their purity and innocence.

Now flee from youthful lusts and pursue righteousness, faith, love and peace, with those who call on the Lord from a pure heart.

—2 Timothy 2:22

That's why we've named this weekend Passport2Purity. The goal of our instruction with our children is not just protecting their virginity, but helping our children protect their purity and innocence. And those two God-given gifts are lost long before intercourse when your preteen begins to experience the sexual response that God designed only for marriage. Ask yourself a couple of questions that helped *us* clarify *our* convictions:

1. Just how far do you want your child to advance toward sexual intimacy before his marriage bed?

2. What level of sexual intimacy do you think God wants your child to experience outside of marriage?

Abstinence is a *part* of the answer. It's just not the *total* answer.

Our culture is robbing far too many Christian parents of their standards, convictions, and courage.

As a result, many of our teens lack the standards and convictions that will protect and lead them through the most tempting and vulnerable period of their entire lives.

We must set our sights high and challenge our children to the highest standard—God's standard. As parents, we want them to arrive at marriage innocent of evil, pure in their sexuality, and with a healthy view of marriage—not encumbered by emotional baggage from sexual mistakes during the teenage years.

God has given your children a beautiful, exquisitely wrapped gift—their innocence—to give to their future spouse on their wedding day. Your job, as a parent, is to guide them in the power of the Holy Spirit through adolescence to maturity, and then to help them maintain the integrity of that gift. Once you make that your goal, it will change the way you think about how you protect and guide your teenager.

WHAT YOU CAN EXPECT

Passport2Purity is a weekend experience consisting of five sessions that feature an audio message and discussion questions. All of the sessions include a special project that will help your preteen learn the concepts even more clearly. This parent's manual will guide you step-by-step as you successfully plan, prepare for, and implement the event. You may be able to plan your weekend getaway quickly and easily, or you may struggle a bit. Press on—it's worth it. Before you know it, you will have a great getaway planned.

When you're on your weekend, if something funny happens, laugh! Let go a little and have fun!

By the way, although it works best to complete this material on a weekend away from your home, it's not necessary to do it all in one weekend. You could complete it over a period of four or five weeks. But we highly recommend the weekend away—it will develop your relationship much more, and your preteen will be more open to discussing these topics away from his normal environment.

Your weekend will not be perfect, but it should be memorable. Expect to have a lot of fun. Prepare to laugh a lot. We've added some humor to the teaching segments to loosen you up at points. When you're on your weekend, if something funny happens, laugh! Let go a little and have fun!

Expect a few awkward moments. These are tough topics to discuss. There may be some sweaty palms—yours and your preteen's. There may be a few embarrassed, blushing faces. These are okay. These are normal. Just keep moving.

Expect a sense of connection. You're not talking just about grades, picking up the clothes on the floor, and setting the table for dinner. You will be talking to your preteen as an emerging adult. Your preteen will appreciate this. Expect to be connected in a new way. Trust us—you'll love it.

WHAT THIS GETAWAY WILL DO FOR YOU AND YOUR PRETEEN

If you work to make this a memorable weekend, you should receive three big benefits. First, it should help you have more intimate conversations with your preteen. It's not easy to initiate these types of conversations when your preteen begins to establish his independence. This experience can set a precedent and help establish you as a parent who wants to stay in touch about the difficult issues teenagers face. Maintaining a strong relationship with your child is the key that will enable you to guide him through the teen years.

Second, this weekend can give your preteen a foundation for beginning to make wise decisions. Now don't get too excited. Growth may come slowly. But with ongoing conversations and repetitive training, your preteen can learn to base his decisions on biblical convictions.

Third, this weekend will provide rich memories. Be sure to bring a camera along to help you remember the fun. You and your preteen will treasure the time you spend together.

THREE IMPORTANT QUESTIONS

How is your relationship with your preteen right now? If words like "cold," "distant," "strained," or "tense" come to mind, this may not be the best time to get away for a weekend. You may want to take a few weeks or months to build your relationship and your communication *before* you go away. Chapter Six contains a survey that will help you to gauge how well you know your child.

Up to this point, how much have you told your child about sex? Be aware that on this weekend we will explain the "birds and the bees." We will share details about the physical and biological processes of sexual reproduction, masturbation, and moral purity. If you have time before this getaway, we recommend two books by Stan and Brenna Jones: *How and When to Tell Your Kids About Sex* and *Facing the Facts* (NavPress).

How strong are your own personal convictions in the areas you will be discussing? After working with thousands of families over the last twenty-five years in ministry, one thing is crystal clear: A parent cannot challenge a child to have a standard the parent doesn't have himself. You will find some thought-provoking questions in Chapter Five. Once again, *Parenting Today's Adolescent* will help you determine your convictions as you raise your teen.

SUGGESTED RESPONSES TO EMBARRASSING QUESTIONS

A parent cannot challenge a child to have a standard the parent doesn't have himself.

The Raineys suggest the following approach for handling embarrassing questions if you were sexually active outside of marriage in the past:

> "... if you did not enter marriage as a virgin and your child asks a pointed question, we recommend that you not give a complete answer—at least for now. Here's a suggested response: 'That's a good question, and someday when you are an adult and more mature, I want to answer you more fully. But for now, that information is off-limits.'
>
> "If your child is not satisfied and persists, you may want to admit, 'I made some mistakes I

really regret'—but not share further details … It's better if children do not know much about the failures of their parents when they were young. Continue to hold up a high standard and don't be a stumbling block (see Romans 14:13)."

Other suggestions given by the Raineys, especially for when your children are older:

"Just say, 'I made some mistakes and bad choices. I'm sorry, but I ignored my parents' instruction,' or 'I did not have a parent who was challenging my standards and calling me to live out convictions based on Scripture.'"

(Suggestions quoted from *Parenting Today's Adolescent*, pages 67-68, Thomas Nelson, Inc., Publishers.)

A SPECIAL WORD FOR SINGLE PARENTS

This resource is specifically designed for a getaway between a father and son or a mother and daughter. If you are a single mom of a son or a single dad of a daughter, there are some things you should consider:

- If I asked my former spouse to do this getaway, would he or she do it?
- Is my former spouse living a Christ-centered life?
- Does my former spouse have a strong

enough relationship with our preteen to conduct this getaway?

If your former spouse is unwilling, or you decide that the better approach is to plan and carry out the getaway yourself, don't worry. You can still have a successful weekend. Use Passport2Purity as it is, and make any adjustments you feel are necessary for your situation.

You might consider planning this weekend with a friend. That way, you can hold each other accountable for decision-making and preparation. Also, if you have other children, you can swap child care as you each take your weekends away.

A SPECIAL WORD FOR ADOPTIVE PARENTS

Barbara and I are adoptive parents, and we realize that these great kids are sometimes sensitive to how things are stated. During this weekend, we will talk about two things that we want you to be prepared for if questions arise. First, I make brief references to how children look like their parents. I do this to demonstrate how you, as a parent, went through the same struggles your preteen will face over the next few years. If questions arise, be prepared to say things like, "You may not look exactly like me, but you're still a Rainey! It's what's on the inside that really matters."

Second, I talk about God's plan for children to be born within a committed marriage relationship. If your child was born outside of one, he could feel like less than God's best—which isn't true. Remind your child that God had a special plan for your family and blessed your home with him.

God Himself set this model for adoption. It's one of His greatest gifts. He tells us through Paul's letter to the church at Galatia that Christ redeemed us "that we might receive the adoption as sons ... and if a son, then an heir to God" (Galatians 4:5b, 7b).

USING PASSPORT2PURITY WITH YOUR OTHER CHILDREN

We know that the purchase of this resource was a commitment for you. As you plan, you may be thinking about the other younger children in your family. You may want to take them on the same type of memorable weekend when they reach the right age. You can order a Passport2Purity replacement kit (consisting of a new *Adventure Journal*, My Passport, and a set of new Adventure Stamps) by contacting us at:

P.O. Box 7111 ◇ Little Rock, AR 72223-7111
1-800-FL-TODAY ◇ FamilyLife.com

WE'D LOVE TO HEAR FROM YOU!

Have you seen God work in your relationship with your son or daughter through Passport2Purity? Tell us the story! Jot us a note to tell us how your getaway went (let us know if we may quote you) and send it to us. We would love to hear from your preteen, too!

FamilyLife Publishing
Attention: Passport2Purity
5800 Ranch Drive
Little Rock, AR 72223

Visit us at:
FamilyLife.com/passport/parent/getaway.html

- Tell us how your getaway went.
- Order Passport2Purity replacement kits.
- Receive future updates on Passport2Purity getaways.

CHAPTER THREE

PLANNING GUIDE:
NINE STEPS TO A GREAT GETAWAY EXPERIENCE

You will want to refer to the Preparation Checklist on page vii.

❑ 1. PRAY. Ask God to give you wisdom as you make plans for this getaway. Pray that He will give you wisdom about how to challenge your teen to establish godly convictions. And ask Him to give your preteen a teachable heart. (See page lxi for suggestions on how to pray for your preteen.)

❑ 2. CHOOSE A DATE. Sit down with your spouse and choose a time that works for both of you. Determine a date a couple of weeks or months away so you have adequate planning time. Check with your family's church, sports, and school calendars. Then, find a creative way to invite your preteen; build anticipation!

❑ 3. FUN! Decide what other activities you'd like to enjoy on Saturday afternoon. Our suggested schedule calls for several hours of free time on Saturday. You want this weekend to be a time of relationship building, so do something your preteen will enjoy. This will help you choose your location. If you both like to fish, for example, you know you'll want to find a hotel or cabin by a lake or river.

A few suggestions:

- ★ Do this somewhere outside your home, where you can be alone together.
- ★ Don't waste time watching television—you can do that any time.
- ★ Plan your outside activities so you'll still have plenty of time to complete the five Passport2Purity sessions.
- ★ Make this a truly memorable activity by choosing something your preteen has always wanted to do, or something that is fun and different from anything you've ever done before. If possible, spend a little more money than instinct usually tells you.
- ★ Don't let the free-time event outgrow the weekend. The activity shouldn't last more than five or six hours. If it does, you'll cut into your instruction and discussion time.
- ★ Make it memorable. Invest in some cheap souvenirs. Take lots of pictures. Laugh with each other.

Here are some possible activities (choose the appropriate one for your child):

- Attend a college or professional sports game.
- Relax at the beach.
- Go fishing.
- Go hiking.
- Go hunting.
- Play 18 holes of golf at a club you've always wanted to play.
- Go canoeing.
- Take a camping trip.
- Visit a unique educational or historical site.
- Go to an amusement park.
- Play tennis.

- Go to the zoo.
- Tour a cave or cavern.
- Ride go-carts or motorcycles.
- Go to a shooting club.
- Take golf lessons.
- Snow ski.
- Water ski.
- Enjoy archery.
- Ice skate.
- Go sailing.
- Pick berries.
- Take a shopping trip to another city.
- Go for a manicure, pedicure, makeover, etc.
- Look for antiques.
- Arrange for a glamour photo session.

❑ 4. **CHOOSE YOUR LOCATION.** *Make the proper arrangements to stay there.* For many of you, this will mean booking a hotel room or perhaps arranging to use a friend's vacation home. We recommend going out of town to a location no more than two hours from home. Just being somewhere different will make the trip special.

❑ 5. **PLAN YOUR MEALS.** Choose restaurants, food, snacks, etc., that you know your preteen will enjoy. And plan a special meal for Saturday night when you will present your preteen with his signed Passport document. This celebration dinner will commemorate a true milestone in your son's or daughter's life!

❑ 6. **REVIEW THE MATERIAL.** In order to be fully prepared to facilitate a Passport2Purity weekend, you must familiarize yourself with the material. Listen to the instructional audio message by Dennis Rainey. Then take your

Bible and pen and read through the note-taking outlines in the *Adventure Journal.* Take time to read the "Make Up Your Mind" discussion questions in each section. And be sure to read through the project instructions in Chapter Four. Listen to the CDs ahead of time to be well prepared.

❑ 7. **GATHER YOUR MATERIALS.**

Projects: These special object lessons are in each session. They will make a big difference in how well your preteen learns and remembers the lessons, and they're fun. You'll find the materials you'll need listed in Chapter Four.

Photos: Place a recent picture of your preteen inside the front cover of his *Adventure Journal.* Make sure it's one he will like.

A second place where you may want to place photos is in Session Three. If possible, find pictures of yourself at different stages of development (pre-school, elementary, preteen, and 20s). Glue photos or color copies over the sketches in this session in the student's *Adventure Journal.* Your child will probably get a big charge out of seeing your own development, but the photos will also help him understand that you can relate to what he is about to go through or is going through currently. If you can't locate pictures of yourself, the sketches can stand alone.

Letters: Following the contents page of the student's *Adventure Journal* are two blank pages. These are for you and your spouse to each write letters to your child. If you're a single parent, you may want to ask a grandparent, another relative, or someone close to your child to write a letter. Your preteen will read the letters at the beginning of the getaway. If you can't write one, please don't worry. There are no written instructions on these pages to indicate what they are for.

- ❑ 8. **PURCHASE A SPECIAL GIFT.** This is an optional part of the weekend experience, but we highly recommend it.

  Gifts are significant. They are bookmarks in time that remind us of smells, sights, words, and special people. We feel that an important part of this weekend getaway is the giving of a gift to your preteen as a memento of the weekend.

  This would be a good occasion for a meaningful gift. For example, many parents give their children a piece of jewelry—ring, bracelet, necklace, etc.—that symbolizes a commitment to moral purity.

  Be sure to be sensitive to your preteen's tastes as you choose a gift. For example, if you love earrings, but your daughter loves bracelets, don't buy her earrings. At the same time, choose a gift that has meaning.

Here are some ideas to stimulate your thinking:

- Leather study Bible (embossed)
- Engraved pocketknife
- Cross necklace
- Jewelry (make sure it's the kind your preteen likes)
- Purity ring
- Music box
- Musical instrument
- Unique piece of clothing
- Wristwatch

- Fine writing instrument
- Piece of a collection (coin, stamp, figurine, stuffed animal, doll, sports card)
- Signed and numbered print for room
- Key chain
- Doorknocker for their room
- A family heirloom with meaning
- Miniature sculpture
- Binoculars
- Begin a toolbox (with hammer, screwdriver set, wrench set)
- Camera
- Easel and paints
- Telescope
- Compass
- Pictures and frames (a frame for snapshots taken on the weekend)
- Leather luggage or make-up case
- Specialty coin
- Ring (pearl, precious stone, signet)
- Personalized stationery
- Address book with name engraved on it
- Sweatshirt with logo of someone or some place special
- Engraved letter opener
- Mug with a special saying on it

❑ 9. **MAKE SURE YOU LEAVE ON TIME!** Don't let yourself get bogged down by last-minute work, or you will start your weekend off on the wrong foot. If possible, leave work early—this will communicate how much you value your child and highlight the importance of this getaway. Stick to your schedule to make the most of your time together.

CHAPTER FOUR

PROJECT PREPARATIONS

You will want to refer to the Preparation Checklist on page vii.

Each of the five sessions includes a project—a special learning exercise designed to help your child more clearly understand a significant point. During the audio message you will hear instructions to stop the CD and complete the project. Afterwards, restart the CD to complete the message.

We are listing in this chapter the ingredients and preparation needed for all the projects so you can prepare ahead of time. You'll notice that *most of these projects require water*, so you may want to carry some with you if you will be in a location where water is not easily accessible. Gather your materials and don't worry—we've made the projects as simple as possible. When it's time for each project, full instructions are written in each session. Rehearse all the projects. The more prepared you are, the more of an impression these object lessons will make.

SESSION ONE PROJECT
"PUZZLED"

OBJECTIVE:

To show your preteen the need to use the Bible as the guide to his life.

WHAT YOU WILL NEED:

★ Two different jigsaw puzzles: one easy, one difficult (100 pieces each)
★ A timer (kitchen timer, digital watch, etc.)
★ A paper sack for student's puzzle
★ A small prize (candy bar, CD, etc.)
★ Paper grocery bag labeled "Project One"

PREPARATION:

★ Cut open the boxes ahead of time.
★ Keep the easy puzzle in the original box. This is yours. Practice if you like.
★ Place the difficult puzzle in the paper sack. (Remove corner and border pieces, if you want.) Leave the box top at home.
★ Place all items in the "Project One" bag.

Your child's *Adventure Journal* does not provide project information. These are your teaching notes.

After the project and written comments, return to the audio message for the conclusion.

SESSION ONE PROJECT
"PUZZLED"

WHAT TO DO:

1. Get your Project One bag.
2. Put both puzzles on a table or on the floor. Take the puzzle *with* the box top, and give the bag of puzzle pieces *without* the box top to your child. Get the prize out.
3. Say, "Each of us has a puzzle. We are going to have a contest to see how much of our puzzles we can complete in five minutes. The one with the most assembled pieces wins. There is one rule. We can't say anything to each other. Ready? Go!" And start the timer.

   If your child objects that he doesn't have the box top to guide him, say something like, "Do as well as you can. You can figure it out!" No matter what kind of objections he raises during the next few minutes, tell him to keep on trying. And don't help him out!
4. Call time when the timer goes off.

REVIEW:

1. Look at the two puzzles together; chances are pretty good that you will be much more successful in completing your puzzle than he was with his. Ask, "Why was it easier for me to put my puzzle together?"
2. Ask, "What do you think was the point of this exercise?" If needed, ask, "How would you compare the Bible to a box top for a puzzle?"

3. Together read the following verses:

   How can a young man keep his way pure?
   By keeping it according to Your word.

   —Psalm 119:9

   Your word is a lamp to my feet and a light to my path.

   —Psalm 119:105

4. Say, "No matter what we do or where we go, God has given us His Word as a guide. It tells us about His love, about what He has done to forgive our sins and give us eternal life, plus it gives us commandments to help us make the different choices we face in life. As we go through this weekend, we're going to learn about the different things the Bible has to say about some of the issues you will be facing in the next few years. The Bible is our box top for all areas of life."

The most important thing I learned from this project was:

Allow time for your preteen to write comments after the project.

SESSION TWO PROJECT
"DIRTY WATER"

OBJECTIVE:

To show your preteen the negative influence of bad friends.

WHAT YOU WILL NEED:

- A clear pitcher with removable top (wide mouth needed to pour in ingredients) or a two-liter cola bottle with the top cut off
- Six clear plastic cups
- Two or three different types of "pollution" (dirt, coffee grounds, food coloring, etc.)
- Approx. 1 1/2 qts. water
- Large spoon (to stir)
- One-gallon plastic bag (to dispose of dirty water)
- Paper grocery bag labeled "Project Two"

PREPARATION:

- Gather dry ingredients and clear containers.
- Keep dry ingredients in separate plastic bags.
- Place all items in the "Project Two" bag.

SESSION TWO PROJECT
"DIRTY WATER"

You will be instructed to pause the CD after point B(2) to complete the project "Dirty Water." After the project, restart CD 1, Track 6.

WHAT TO DO:

1. Get your Project Two bag.
2. Direct your preteen to pour water into all six cups.
3. Ask him to put "pollution" (mixed earlier) into three of the cups.
4. Instruct your child to pour one glass of water into the empty pitcher. Say, "This water represents you. Let's say that you are trying to live a life that is pleasing to God. You want to obey your parents, and you want to obey what God tells you in the Bible."
5. Tell your preteen to pour the other two glasses of clear water into the pitcher. Say, "These two glasses represent 'good' friends. What happens when you pour the water into the pitcher? (The water remains clear.) What do you think this signifies? (These friends aren't trying to make you do bad things. Your life is still pleasing to God.)"
6. Now ask your preteen to pour in the "pollution" from one of the glasses. Instruct your child to stir or shake the pitcher to mix up all the water. Say, "These other glasses have junk in them. They represent friends who do not have a good influence on you. See how a bad friend pollutes the whole group?"
7. Instruct your preteen to pour "pollution" into the other two glasses. Ask, "In what ways does a bad friend affect you?" (He tries to get you to disobey parents, to be rebellious, to do things that are wrong, etc.)

Remember—your child does not have any project instructions in his *Adventure Journal.*

8. Reread the memory verses for this lesson, 1 Corinthians 15:33-34a. Work on memorizing them.

CLEAN UP:

Do not pour the contents of the pitcher down the sink!

Allow time for your preteen to write comments.

The most important thing I learned from this project was:

SESSION THREE PROJECT
"BURNED UP"

OBJECTIVE:

To show your child the need to protect his innocence.

WHAT YOU WILL NEED:

- A box of wooden safety matches
- A glass of water
- Paper grocery bag labeled "Project Three"

PREPARATION:

- Place matchbox and a glass or plastic cup in the "Project Three" bag.

SESSION THREE PROJECT
"BURNED UP"

WHAT TO DO:

1. Get your Project Three bag.
2. Direct your daughter to strike one of the matches to ignite it; then blow it out. Tell her to try to light the match again the same way. Ask, "Why won't it light?"
3. Ask, "What do you think this exercise has to do with the subject of sex?" After allowing your daughter to answer, explain that we can only lose our innocence and our virginity one time.
4. Now have her place a second, unlit match in the glass of water, and keep it there. Finally, tell her to light another match and then try to light the match in the glass of water with the lighted match. Of course, it's impossible. Say, "God's desire is that you protect your innocence until you are married. If you draw near to God, He will supply the wisdom and strength to do what He requires. What you need to do is stay away from any flame that could light your match, so to speak. In the next lesson, we'll talk more about what that means."

The most important thing I learned from this project was:

Allow time for your preteen to write comments.

SESSION FOUR PROJECT
"LEAKY BALLOON"

OBJECTIVE:

To show your preteen how seemingly small decisions about boundaries can cause him to lose his innocence.

WHAT YOU WILL NEED:

- A balloon that is strong and large enough so that when you fill it with water and pierce it with a needle it won't burst, but will dribble out a drop or two, and if squeezed, will shoot out a stream of water. We strongly suggest buying helium grade latex balloons from a party store or florist. Buy extras in case one bursts.
- A thin, sharp needle
- Colorful string to thread needle (for safety)
- Water (to fill balloon)
- Roll of transparent tape
- Paper grocery bag labeled "Project Four"

PREPARATION:

- Place all objects in "Project Four" bag.

Pause the message after point C(5) and begin working on the project "Leaky Balloon."

Challenge your preteen to respect and protect the purity of others while guarding his own purity.

NOTE: After the project, continue the audio message. [CD 4, Track 1] Dennis will refer to another project. Get out your Project Four bag. Instruct your preteen to glue together two sheets of paper (different colors), pressing them flat. Set this aside for Session Five.

SESSION FOUR PROJECT
"LEAKY BALLOON"

WHAT TO DO:

Note: If you've had problems with the balloon popping while practicing this experiment, place a piece of clear tape on the surface of the balloon after adding the water. Pierce the balloon through the tape.

1. Get your Project Four bag.
2. Fill the balloon with water, then hold it up. Say, "Let's pretend this water balloon is filled with your sexual purity and innocence. This is all that you have. How much of it would you like to save for your spouse on your wedding night?" Let him answer.
3. Continue: "Let's say that someone comes to you and just wants a little kiss—your first kiss and just a little bit of your innocence." Hold the balloon up and pierce it with the needle so that a teensy drop comes out (squeeze it lightly if necessary). Say, "The person says to you, 'It's just a little drop. Just an ever-so-teensy drop. You'll never miss it.'"
4. Pierce the balloon again with the needle. Say, "And then someone else comes along and just wants a little droplet." Pierce it two or three more times. "And after that, let's say that person liked what she got and wants even more of your innocence, so now you've lost several drops."

5. Pierce the balloon several more times. “Then let’s say you really fall for someone special and you decide it’s okay to give even more of your purity and innocence away.” Squeeze the balloon so more water squirts out. “Unfortunately, you break up with this person and move on.” Keep squeezing until there’s nothing left.
6. “Finally, you’re older and you find the person you want to marry and spend the rest of your life with.” Hold up the empty balloon. “What’s going to happen to innocence and purity? How much do you have left when you marry?” Let him answer. “And how would you have lost your purity and innocence—all at once or little by little?” Again, let your preteen answer and conclude by saying, “That is how young people today are losing one of the most precious gifts that they can give to another human being, and they start by giving it away a drop at a time. Then they give away even more, and the holes get larger and it’s no longer drops, but a small stream. Don’t give away your innocence. Save it for your wedding night.”

The most important thing I learned from this project was:

Allow your preteen time to write comments.

SESSION FIVE PROJECT
"ALL GLUED UP"

OBJECTIVE:

To show your preteen one of the dangers of becoming too attached to someone of the opposite sex.

WHAT YOU WILL NEED:

- At least six sheets of construction paper—two different colors (three red and three yellow)
- White school glue (not a glue stick)
- Paper grocery bag labeled "Project Five"

PREPARATION:

- Place all items in the "Project Five" bag.

Continue to train your child and stay involved through the years.

SESSION FIVE PROJECT
"All GLUED UP"

WHAT TO DO:

1. Get your Project Five bag.
2. Direct your preteen to take two different-colored sheets of paper out of the bag. Have him brush the two sheets against each other several times. Say, "A young man and young lady can have fun spending time together in casual friendship. And, just like these two sheets, they stay complete and new as long as they don't start forming exclusive attachments."
3. Pull out two more different-colored sheets. Say, "Based on my own experience and what Dennis Rainey explained, I want to warn you about creating these exclusive attachments in a relationship. Watch closely. Let's say you risk getting too close to someone of the opposite sex. You spend time talking on the phone (apply a dab of glue to the paper), hang out together as a couple at youth activities (another dab), start chatting on the Internet (dab), sit alone together at lunch (dab), ride alone in the car (dab), hold hands (dab), pass notes to each other (dab), start dating (dab), etc., etc., etc. (dab, dab, dab, dab)." Now, put the two sheets flat together so they are glued. Say, "These exclusive attachments start to glue you together. You enjoy being together and become attached to each other."

After this project, ask your preteen to suggest ways to avoid exclusive attachments. Share your views on acceptable and unacceptable ways to spend time together with the opposite sex. Ask your preteen's view and discuss the dangers in some of these situations.

4. Now, ask your child to take the two sheets and pull them apart. Say, "Notice that if you pull them apart after a short time, they're not destroyed, but they are still a little messed up, stained from the remnants of the glue. Exclusive attachments do that."
5. Finally, tell your preteen to take the two sheets that were glued together at the end of Session Four and pull them apart. Say, "If your exclusive relationship goes on for a while, you risk destroying each other (physically, emotionally, and spiritually) and your lives will never be the same again. You are no longer clean and new for your future husband or wife."
6. Say, "The wisest route to take when you are young is not to get attached to one person. Chances are you will not marry for another 10 years or so. Why worry about finding a girlfriend right now? This is the time to learn how to get along with the opposite sex—not to act like you're married."

The most important thing I learned from this project was:

Allow your preteen time to write comments.

CHAPTER FIVE

CLARIFYING YOUR OWN CONVICTIONS:
WHAT DO YOU REALLY BELIEVE?

INTRODUCTION

If you have not worked out your own biblical convictions about peer pressure, sexual purity, and dating, you will have a difficult time challenging your preteen to clear standards. This chapter is designed to help you and your spouse wrestle with and define what you, as a couple, truly believe.

Our oldest daughter, Ashley, took a speech class in high school. Occasionally, the teacher would ask one student to come up to the front of the room and sit in the "hot seat." The other students could ask any question they wanted of the person in the hot seat. Well we're putting you in the hot seat right now! It's important for you to think through some of the questions and issues that you'll deal with on your Passport2Purity getaway. Take some time away from the interruptions of life and answer the following questions. Be honest with yourself and God. We hope these questions prepare you for any hot seat sitting you may have to do on your getaway.

Under each topic, we suggest you answer the questions individually and then discuss your answers with your spouse. (If you are single, we suggest finding another parent with whom you can discuss these questions.) You will find this time well spent. You'll have some great discussions, and you will build some solid family values you can pass on to your children.

The following questions are adapted from *Parenting Today's Adolescent.* For help in thinking through your convictions, we recommend that you read *Parenting Today's Adolescent* before your getaway, if possible. Reading it after your getaway will also be very valuable to you.

PEER PRESSURE

1. How often do you compare what you have with what others have? Are you a person who tries to keep up with the Joneses with things like your car, home furnishings, clothing, club memberships, gadgets, and so on?

2. Would you describe yourself as a people pleaser? How might that influence your child's reactions to peer pressure?

3. How is the quality of your relationship with your child? The quality of your relationship will be the determining factor in how significant peer influence will be in his life. How are you doing at making him feel a sense of belonging and love? Is your home a harbor of safety in a hostile world?

4. How do you view the impact of peer relationships on your child? What role will you take in challenging your preteen with regard to positive and negative friendships?

5. How involved will you be in influencing or controlling your child's relationships? Will you meet his friends? How much time will you spend getting to know his friends and how will you accomplish this?

SEXUAL PURITY

1. What is the purpose for sex?

2. What standards do you want to challenge your teen to in the following areas?

   - Being alone with the opposite sex
   - Holding hands
   - Hugs
   - Kissing
   - Passionate hugging and kissing
   - Lying down while passionately hugging and kissing
   - Touching below the neck
   - Touching below the waist
   - Taking clothes off
   - Intercourse

3. As you look at the list in question two, where do you think your preteen will draw the line with the opposite sex?

4. Looking at the same list, where do you want to challenge your preteen to draw the line with the opposite sex?

5. How much physical intimacy do you think God intended for us to experience outside of the marriage relationship? Stated another way: How much sexual activity do you think you should experience prior to marriage?

DATING

1. What dating standards did you follow when you were a teenager? If your child could repeat your dating experience, would you let him?

2. If you regret mistakes you made in your own dating behavior prior to marriage, have you confessed them to God and claimed His forgiveness? If not, do so now and do not allow past sins to prevent you from setting standards of holiness and purity for your preteen.

3. What rules and boundaries will you set for your preteen concerning the following issues?

   - When to date
   - Whom to date
   - Acceptable kinds of dates
   - Telephone calls
   - Internet communications

4. What do you need to teach your preteen about how to treat the opposite sex?

5. What do you need to teach your preteen about how to find a spouse?

CHAPTER SIX

HOW WELL DO YOU KNOW YOUR PRETEEN?

It's important to have a good relationship already established with your preteen before you go on your Passport2Purity getaway. The better you know your child, the more he will listen to you when you discuss topics like peer pressure, sex, and dating.

The following questionnaire was written by Miriam Neff, a high school counselor who knows the issues preteens and teens struggle through. More than that, she has raised four teenagers. As you go through these questions, you'll begin to see how close, or how distant, your relationship is with your child. If you don't know all the answers, fill in what you can and use the others as conversation starters on your drive to your getaway location.

NOTE: If you find you don't know at least half of the answers, we strongly suggest you postpone your Passport2Purity getaway. Take a few weeks to do some intentional relationship building—take walks, go to breakfast, do fun activities, etc. This effort will greatly impact the success of your getaway and beyond.

1. Who is your preteen's best friend?

2. What color would he like for the walls in his bedroom?

3. Who is your preteen's greatest hero?

4. What embarrasses your preteen most?

5. What is your preteen's biggest fear?

6. What is his favorite type of music?

7. What person outside the immediate family has most influenced the life of your preteen?

8. What is his favorite school subject?

9. What is his least favorite school subject?

10. What has your preteen done that he feels most proud of?

11. What is your preteen's biggest complaint about the family?

12. What sport does your preteen most enjoy?

13. What is his favorite TV program?

14. What is your preteen's favorite Internet site?

15. What really makes your preteen angry?

16. What would your preteen like to be when he grows up?

17. What chore does your preteen like least?

18. What three foods does your preteen like most?

19. What is your preteen's most prized possession?

20. What is his favorite family occasion?

21. What activity did your preteen enjoy most last weekend?

PRAYING FOR YOUR PRETEEN

One of the most important lessons Barbara and I have learned as we've parented six children is that we need to pray for them continually. We believe in the prayer of helpless parents, who come humbly before God with the realization that He is the One who ultimately controls their destiny.

Below we have listed 26 ways you can pray for your preteen. You can use these not only to prepare for your Passport2Purity getaway, but also as a guide for prayer throughout his preteen and teenage years.

1. Pray that God will protect your preteen's innocence.
2. Pray that God will bring godly friends into your preteen's life.
3. Pray that your preteen won't forget how to laugh.
4. Pray that God will draw your preteen into a relationship with Him or deepen the relationship that's already established.
5. Pray that God will bring other godly adults into your preteen's life.
6. Pray that your preteen will be grounded in the spiritual disciplines of Bible study, prayer, and worship.
7. Pray that your preteen will learn to love the unlovely (reach out to other kids).
8. Pray that God will bring about tests of character in your preteen's life to help him learn how to stand strong in his convictions.
9. Pray that your preteen will develop humility.
10. Pray that you will catch your preteen in sin in order to have opportunities to train him.
11. Pray that your preteen will develop a larger peer group of believers that can have its own identity—enjoying music, parties, and memories together.

12. Pray that intellectual understanding of the changes in your preteen's body will give him cause to praise God for His glorious creation.

13. Pray that your preteen will respect and treat the opposite sex in a biblical manner.

14. Pray that your preteen will develop his own convictions about what he watches, listens to, and reads.

15. Pray that your preteen will learn self-control.

16. Pray that if your preteen is lying to you, God will allow you to catch him in that lie. Pray also that God will give him the courage to follow through with restitution and repentance.

17. Pray that your preteen will not give in to the temptation to use drugs or alcohol.

18. Pray that your preteen will develop a loving and caring relationship with his siblings.

19. Pray that your preteen will learn how to manage his anger.

20. Pray that your preteen will learn how to control his tongue.

21. Pray that God will protect your preteen's mind from being polluted by pornographic images and ideas.

22. Pray that your preteen will not develop an attachment and preoccupation with material things.

23. Pray that God will keep the communication lines open between you and your preteen during the teenage years.

24. Pray that your preteen will develop biblical convictions.

25. Pray that your preteen will stand strong when peers pressure him to do something contrary to those convictions.

26. Pray that your preteen will begin to understand God's mission for his life.

So You're About to Be a Teenager

by Dennis and Barbara Rainey
with Samuel Rainey and Rebecca Rainey

Recognize warning signs of pre-adolescence and prepare your preteen for challenging times by:

- dispelling fears
- answering questions
- outlining traps

Purposefully guide your preteen with truth and successfully navigate the "mind" field! Available at **FamilyLife.com.**

Do you have more than one child that you would like to take on a Passport2Purity weekend? There is no need to buy another complete resource pack. All you need is this replacement pack, which contains:

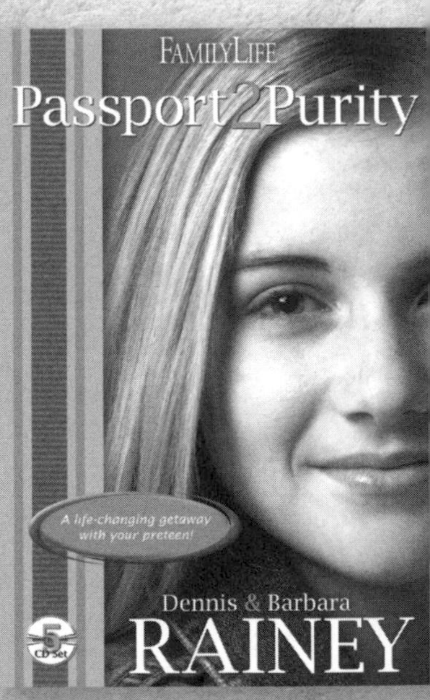

- An *Adventure Journal* (student manual)
- A commemorative passport
- Transparent seals to mark commitments made during the weekend
- Does NOT include audio CDs

Visit **FamilyLife.com/passport** for more information about this exciting resource!

Passport2Purity®

Section Two
Adventure Journal

With Instructions for Parents

We'd love to hear from you!

Jot us a note about how your Passport2Purity adventure went.

FAMILYLIFE
Publishing®

Attention: Passport2Purity
5800 Ranch Drive
Little Rock, AR 72223

Please visit: FamilyLife.com/passport

Parent's Note: Just before your getaway, fill out this page in your preteen's *Adventure Journal*.

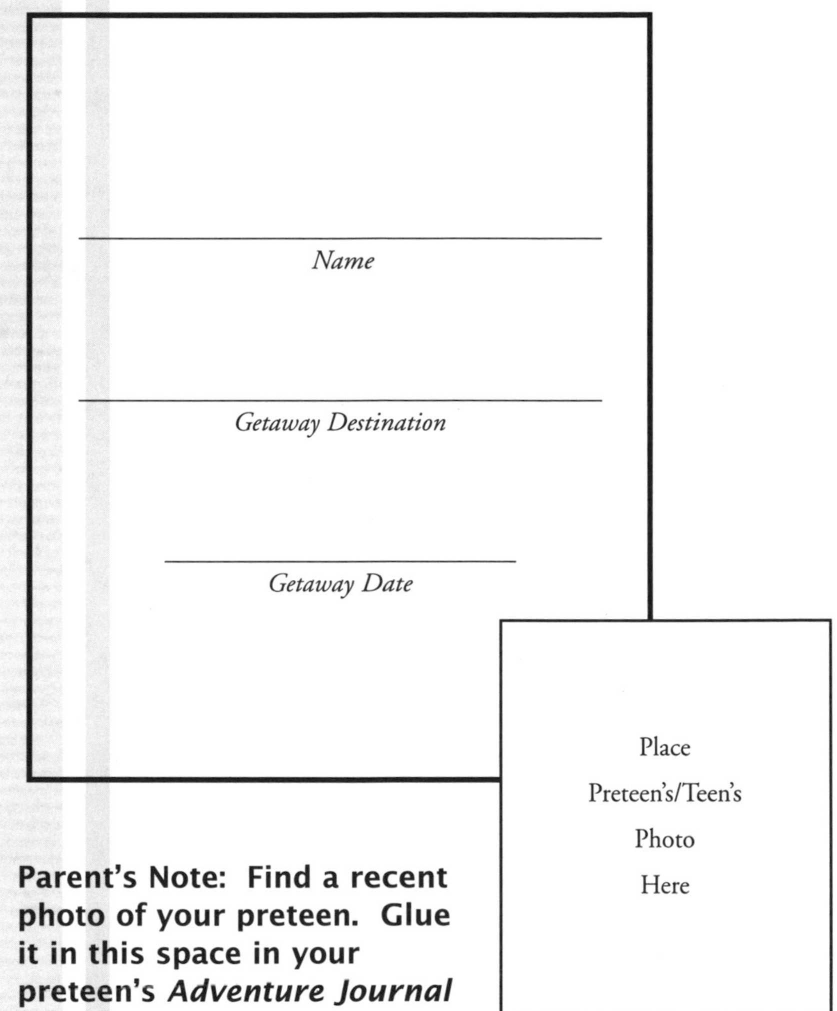

Name
Getaway Destination
Getaway Date
Place
Preteen's/Teen's
Photo
Here

Parent's Note: Find a recent photo of your preteen. Glue it in this space in your preteen's *Adventure Journal*

Tour Guide
Adventure Journal
With Instructions for Parents

TABLE OF CONTENTS

Letter from You to Your Preteen

This page and the next page are blank in your child's *Adventure Journal*. It will really enhance your time together and provide a source of ongoing encouragement if you take the time before your getaway to write him letters on his two blank pages. If, for some reason, you can't write the letters, please don't worry. There are no references to these letters in your child's *Adventure Journal*.

Preparation

- Before you write your letter, spend some time thinking about and praying for your child—how God has gifted him, his strengths, what you appreciate about him, how you see God using him, and why he makes you proud. Take notes and make these the basis for your letter.
- You may find it helpful to discuss your observations with your spouse, a grandparent, or a friend who knows your child well.

Writing the Letter

- Draft: Write out your letter on a separate sheet. When you have the letter the way you want it, rewrite it in your preteen's *Adventure Journal*.
- Personal: Share your feelings in a natural way. This needs to be your own style of communicating.
- A Milestone: Recognize that he is growing up. Indicate that he is becoming a young man and that you are excited about the teen years and the future ahead of him.

- Appreciation: Share how proud you are of him and let him know how much you appreciate him.
- Affirmation: Highlight some key strengths, gifts, and talents that you see God developing in his life.
- Mission: Give him a sense that God has created him with a unique purpose and mission in life. Explain that his God-given strengths and gifts, along with his sincere desire to love and serve God, are key to his fulfilling his mission.
- Excitement: Share your excitement about this special getaway together, as well as your desire to have a great time of fun and discussion about some very important areas of life.
- Commitment and Love: Indicate that, with the help of the Holy Spirit, these next few years in his life can and will be a great time of preparation for adulthood. Emphasize your (and your spouse's) personal commitment to train and support him through this time. Finally, express your unconditional love for him.

Presenting the Letter(s)

Give your preteen his *Adventure Journal* at your kick-off dinner on Friday. Ask him to open to pages F and G to read the letter(s). If you are able to do so, it might add a deeper dimension to your time if you read the letter(s) aloud to him. A hug, handshake, or other affirming touch would be very appropriate if your child is comfortable with this.

Did you remember to feed the dog?
I thought you fed the dog!

SESSION 1

Topics:

* Priority of God's Word
* Expectations for the weekend
* Rules for your getaway
* Watch out for those traps!
* Authorities in your life

Memory Verses:

* Colossians 1:18
* Psalm 119:105

Project:

"Puzzled" — is your prep done?

Start the CD player for Session One: "Blastoff." [CD 1, Track 1]

Instruct your preteen to write the memory verse in the box provided in his *Adventure Journal.*

NOTE: Boxes are empty.

Children, obey your parents in the Lord, for this is right. Honor your father and mother (which is the first commandment with a promise), so that it may be well with you, and that you may live long on the earth.
—Ephesians 6:1-3

Memory Verse #1: Colossians 1:18

He is also head of the body, the church; and He is the beginning, the firstborn from the dead, so that He Himself will come to have first place in everything.

A. Expectations for the weekend:

1. Have ___fun___.
2. Be ready to ___honestly answer___ tough questions.
3. We hope you will ___remember___ this weekend for the rest of your life!

B. We have some ___rules___ for you.

1. ___Laugh___ a lot.
2. ___Listen___ to each other.
3. Keep everything ___confidential___ when it's over.
4. Stay on your ___schedule___.

C. Watch out for those ______traps______!

1. Every ______teenager______ faces traps.

2. These traps can ______ensnare______ you.

Be sure your preteen reads the verse(s) in the margins. You may want to ask him the meaning of each one.

3. To avoid traps, you need to make wise ______choices______ based on your personal ______convictions______.

D. There are ______authorities______ to whom you should listen.

The teaching of the wise is a fountain of life, to turn aside from the snares of death.
—Proverbs 13:14

1. Your parents have the responsibility to ______guide______ you through the traps you will face as a teenager.

2. Teachers, coaches, youth group leaders, and others will ______teach______ you the Word of God and ______strengthen______ the convictions you gain from your parents.

3. Your ultimate authority is God and His Word.

Memory Verse #2:
Psalm 119:105

Your word is a lamp to my feet and a light to my path.

After the memory verse, you will be instructed to stop the CD and complete the project "Puzzled" on the next page. When you are finished, restart the CD.
[CD 1, Track 2]

Your child's *Adventure Journal* does not provide project information. These are your teaching notes.

After the project and written comments, return to the audio message for the conclusion.

SESSION ONE PROJECT
"PUZZLED"

OBJECTIVE:

To show your preteen the need to use the Bible as the guide to his life.

WHAT YOU WILL NEED:

- ★ Two different jigsaw puzzles: one easy, one difficult (100 pieces each)
- ★ A timer (kitchen timer, digital watch, etc.)
- ★ A paper sack for student's puzzle
- ★ A small prize (candy bar, CD, etc.)
- ★ Paper grocery bag labeled "Project One"

PREPARATION:

- ★ Cut open the boxes ahead of time.
- ★ Keep the easy puzzle in the original box. This is yours. Practice if you like.
- ★ Place the difficult puzzle in the paper sack. (Remove corner and border pieces, if you want.) Leave the box top at home.
- ★ Place all items in the "Project One" bag.
- ★ See pages xlii-xliii for project instructions and a script.

Allow your preteen time to write comments.

The most important thing I learned from this project was:

ICE BREAKERS!

Your child does not have the Part One questions. Try to initiate discussion. Don't settle for one-word answers.

Part One: Questions for You

{No worries! These are for fun!}

1. *If there is one school subject you wish you would never have to study again, what is it? Why? What's so bad about it?*
2. *If I could give you a time machine ticket to anywhere in the world, past or present, where would you go? Why? What would you do? Whom would you want to take with you?*
3. *If you could meet someone famous (sports, entertainment, politics, etc.), whom would it be? Why? What questions would you ask him or her? What kinds of things would you want to do?*

Part Two: Questions for Your Parent!

1. *What's the dumbest thing you ever said to a teacher? What happened to you? Why do you remember saying it?*
2. *If you could change one thing about how you spend your time every day right now, what would it be? Why? What could you do about it?*
3. *If the house were on fire and you knew the whole family was safe, what one thing would you try to bring out of the house with you? Why? Is there a story behind this item that you can tell me?*

To mark the completion of this session, take out one of the Adventure Stamps included in the Passport2Purity box. Place it in your child's *Adventure Journal* on top of the seal image at the end of Session One. You should sign and date his *Adventure Journal* page.

Congratulations!

You have completed Session One of Passport2Purity!

SESSION 2

Running with the Herd

Topics:

* What is peer pressure?
* What's so bad about giving in?
* How to avoid running with the herd
* What to look for in a good friend

Memory Verses:

* 1 Corinthians 15:33-34a

Project:

"Dirty Water"—is your prep done?

Start the CD player for Session Two: "Running With the Herd." [CD 1, Track 3]

You will be instructed to stop the message so your child can write down his best friends' names. When he is finished, restart the message again. [CD 1, Track 4]

Pause CD. (Mom or Dad, tenaciously guard your relationship with your child! This will be the determining factor in how he handles peer pressure later on. Don't relinquish your authority to peers!) [Restart on CD 1, Track 5]

Instruct your preteen to write the memory verse in the box.

A. What is peer pressure?

Peer pressure is when friends or acquaintances begin to influence you to do what's right or to do something wrong. Peer pressure isn't necessarily good or bad—it can be either one.

My best friends:

1. ___Everyone___ is susceptible to peer pressure.

2. Even ___adults___ are influenced by peers.

3. Peer pressure will ___test___ your convictions.

B. What's so ___bad___ about giving in to peer pressure?

1. The ___Bible___ tells us that "bad company corrupts good morals."

Memory Verses #3:
1 Corinthians 15:33, 34a

Do not be deceived:
"Bad company corrupts good morals."
Become sober-minded as you ought, and stop sinning ...

2. Your friends can be a ___corrosive___ influence if they do not share your convictions.

SESSION TWO PROJECT
"DIRTY WATER"

You will be instructed to pause the CD after point B(2) to complete the project "Dirty Water." After the project, restart CD 1, Track 6.

OBJECTIVE:

To show your preteen the negative influence of bad friends.

WHAT YOU WILL NEED:

- A clear pitcher with removable top (wide mouth needed to pour in ingredients) or a two-liter cola bottle with the top cut off
- Six clear plastic cups
- Two or three different types of "pollution" (dirt, coffee grounds, food coloring, etc.)
- Approx. 1 1/2 qts. water
- Large spoon (to stir)
- One-gallon plastic bag (to dispose of dirty water)
- Paper grocery bag labeled "Project Two"

Remember—your child does not have any project instructions in his *Adventure Journal*.

PREPARATION:

- Gather dry ingredients and clear containers.
- Keep dry ingredients in separate plastic bags.
- Place all items in the "Project Two" bag.
- See pages xlv-xlvi for project instructions and a script.

The most important thing I learned from this project was:

Allow your preteen time to write comments.

He is also head of the body, the church; and He is the beginning, the firstborn from the dead, so that He Himself will come to have first place in everything.
—Colossians 1:18

You may want to ask your preteen the meaning of these verses.

C. How can I avoid running with the wrong herd?

1. You need a __personal relationship__ with __Jesus Christ__ to be able to withstand peer pressure.

2. You need to know __who__ you are and __why__ you are here.

3. You need to __make up your mind__ in advance about what you are going to do before facing the temptations of your teenage years.

4. You need to know what to look for in a __good__ __friend__.

   a. **Brain:** What do they __think__ about and what do they know?

   b. **Eyes:** What do they __watch__, what do they __read__, what do they __look at__? Are they committed to God's way?

   c. **Mouth:** What do they __talk__ about? What kind of language do they use?

d. **Heart:** Are they committed to ____Jesus____ ____Christ____?

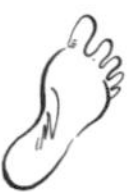

e. **Feet:** ____Where____ do they go to spend time? Do they walk on the "narrow path"?

Remember:
Your parents are great friends and good judges of character.

For we are His workmanship, created in Christ Jesus for good works, which God prepared beforehand so that we would walk in them.
—Ephesians 2:10

When the message is finished, stop the CD and begin working on the "Make Up Your Mind" questions on the next page.

This material is in your child's *Adventure Journal.* Read and discuss it together.

MAKE UP YOUR MIND

Part One: Questions for You

DECIDE IN ADVANCE: You and three others are spending the night at your best friend's house. One friend opens his bag and pulls out a six-pack of beer that he smuggled in. Everyone begins drinking except you, and they begin to pressure you to do the same. "One drink isn't going to hurt you," they say. "So what if your parents tell you that you can't drink alcohol? Do you think they always obeyed their own parents? Do you think they never drank alcohol when they were teenagers?"

What do you do?

What are some things you think you'll be pressured by your friends to do during the next few years?

Why do you think it's important to choose good friends?

Part Two: Questions for Your Parent!

DECIDE IN ADVANCE: There is only one month until school is out for the summer. Your preteen comes home from school one day and asks, "Where are we going to go for vacation this year?"

"I think we're going to go camping in the mountains for a week," you reply.

Your child frowns. "We did that last year. Why can't we go to Disney World? A lot of my friends are going there this summer, and I've never been there!"

"But we can't afford to go to Disney World," you say.

"That's what you say every year. Our vacations are so boring!"

You'd like to go to Disney World as well. You wish you had as much money as many of the families in your area, but you don't. In fact, the only way you could go to Disney World would be to charge the whole trip to a credit card and hope you could find the money to pay for it in the future.

What do you do?

When you were a teenager, did you do anything as a result of peer pressure that you regret now? Talk about it.

What types of peer pressure situations do you face as an adult?

Warning: Avoid discussing significant moral failures with your child, especially in the area of sex. Adolescents need role models, not an excuse to sin. Refer to page xxix in your Tour Guide for suggested responses.

Part Three: Questions for You

What do you think you need to do to resist peer pressure?

What are some ways you could have a positive influence on your friends?

Congratulations!

You have completed Session Two of Passport2Purity!

GIVING CHRIST FIRST PLACE IN EVERYTHING
Passport 2Purity
COLOSSIANS ONE:EIGHTEEN

Take one of the Adventure Stamps and place it in your child's *Adventure Journal* at the end of Session Two. You should sign and date his page.

SESSION 3

For Daughters

Topics:

* Change is inevitable
* Bombarded by hormones
* Body changes
* Sexual intercourse
* What the Bible says about sex
* Relating to young men

Memory Verses:

* 1 Corinthians 6:18-20

Project:

"Burned Up" — is your prep done?

Start the CD for Session Three: "Growing to Sexual Maturity for Daughters." [CD 2, Track 1]

Mom, if possible, find four pictures (2 1/4" x 2" or smaller) of yourself at different stages of development (pre-school, elementary, preteen, and 20s). Glue them over the sketches on page 17 of your daughter's *Adventure Journal*. You may want to use color copies of your photos. If you can't locate pictures of yourself, the sketches can stand alone.

A. ____Change____ is inevitable.

B. Your body is being bombarded by __hormones__.

C. Your body is ___changing___.

1. As you enter into adolescence, your ___breasts___ will grow ___larger___ and rounder.

2. New <u>hair</u> will grow on your body.

3. You will have your first <u>menstrual</u> cycle.

4. Your pelvic bone structure and body fat will <u>change</u>.

5. You will develop an <u>interest</u> in <u>young men</u>.

PAUSE FOR A BREAK.

Likewise, I want women to adorn themselves with proper clothing, modestly and discreetly.
—1 Timothy 2:9a

You may want to ask your daughter the meaning of this verse.

It's okay to smile, blush, giggle, or laugh together. In fact, this may ease the moment.

You will be instructed to pause the message and take a short break before the sex talk.

If your daughter has questions about sexually transmitted diseases that you can't answer, we recommend the book *Human Sexuality: A Christian Perspective* (from the Learning About Sex Series), by Roger Sonnenberg.

See your Tour Guide, page xxix, for other recommended books about sex.

[Start CD 2, Track 2]

God blessed them; and God said to them, "Be fruitful and multiply, and fill the earth, and subdue it."
—Genesis 1:28a

You may want to ask your daughter the meaning of this verse.

D. What is ____sexual intercourse____?

E. What does the ____Bible____ say about sex?

1. Your sexuality is a marvelous ____creation____ of God.

2. God designed sex within marriage so that ____children____ could come into the world.

3. God designed sex within marriage so that you could experience ____closeness____ with your ____husband____.

4. God designed sex in marriage to bring you a great deal of ___pleasure___.

When the message is finished, stop the CD and begin working on the project "Burned Up" and the "Make Up Your Mind" questions.

F. Relating to young men.

Jot down key messages and your thoughts during the audio message.

Important note! At the end of this message, Dennis will tell you it's time for your project. As indicated in Section One of your Tour Guide, we have included a short exhortation specifically for girls on the subject of masturbation. [CD 2, Track 3] Continue to play the CD until the end of this message to listen to it. If you decided you don't want your daughter to hear this now, stop the CD and move directly to the project "Burned Up."

Memory Verses #4:
1 Corinthians 6:18-20

Flee immorality. Every other sin that a man commits is outside the body, but the immoral man sins against his own body. Or do you not know that your body is a temple of the Holy Spirit who is in you, whom you have from God, and that you are not your own? For you have been bought with a price: therefore glorify God in your body.

STOP THE CD

Instruct your daughter to write the memory verse in the box.

SESSION THREE PROJECT
"BURNED UP"

OBJECTIVE:

To show your child the need to protect his innocence.

WHAT YOU WILL NEED:

- A box of wooden safety matches
- A glass of water
- Paper grocery bag labeled "Project Three"

PREPARATION:

- Place matchbox and a glass or plastic cup in the "Project Three" bag.
- See page xlviii for project instructions and a script.

The most important thing I learned from this project was:

Allow your preteen time to write comments.

MAKE UP YOUR MIND

If you sense your daughter needs to talk more as you are working through these questions, ask her if she has any questions she'd like to discuss about sex or if there's anything she has wondered about.

Part One: Sexual Maturity Questionnaire

What is your biggest question or fear about your body and how you are developing?

How do you think other preteens/teens view your physical and emotional maturity?

What do you think is the purpose of sex?

What does the Bible say about sex?

Before today, what percent of everything you had learned about sex came from the following? (The total should equal 100 percent.)

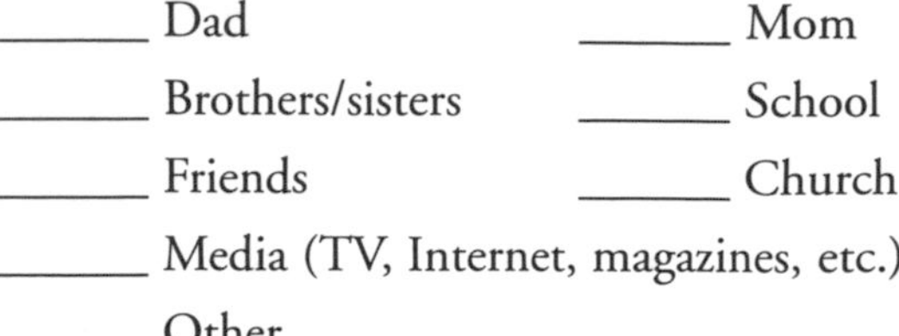

______ Dad
______ Mom
______ Brothers/sisters
______ School
______ Friends
______ Church
______ Media (TV, Internet, magazines, etc.)
______ Other

With whom would you prefer to talk about sex?

Place one of the Adventure Stamps in your child's *Adventure Journal* at the end of Session Three. You should sign and date her page.

Part Two: Discussion

With your parent, talk about your answers to each of the questions in the Sexual Maturity Questionnaire.

Congratulations!

You have completed Session Three of Passport2Purity!

SESSION 3

Growing to Sexual Maturity

For Sons

Topics:
* Change is inevitable
* Bombarded by hormones
* Body changes
* Sexual intercourse
* What the Bible says about sex
* Relating to young women

Memory Verses:
* 1 Corinthians 6:18-20

Project:
"Burned Up" — is your prep done?

Passport2Purity®

Start the CD for Session Three: "Growing to Sexual Maturity for Sons." [CD 3, Track 1]

Dad, if possible, find four pictures (2 1/4" x 2" or smaller) of yourself at different stages of development (pre-school, elementary, preteen, and 20s). Glue them over the sketches on page 25 of your son's *Adventure Journal*. You may want to use color copies of your photos. If you can't locate pictures of yourself, the sketches can stand alone.

A. ___Change___ is inevitable.

B. Your body is being bombarded by ___hormones___.

C. Your body is ___changing___.

1. Your ___voice___ will deepen.

2. You will begin to grow ___body___ and ___facial hair___. You will also begin to have body ___odor___.

3. You will grow in __height__ and in muscle __bulk__.

4. Your __penis__ will grow bigger and change in shape.

It's okay to smile, blush, giggle, or laugh together. In fact, this may ease the moment.

5. You will develop an __interest__ in __young__ __women__.

PAUSE FOR A BREAK.

You will be instructed to pause the message and take a short break before the sex talk.

…our son has …estions about …exually …ransmitted diseases that you can't answer, we recommend the book *Human Sexuality: A Christian Perspective* (from the Learning About Sex Series), by Roger Sonnenberg.

See your Tour Guide, page xxix, for other recommended books about sex.

[Start CD 3, Track 2]

D. What is ____sexual intercourse____?

E. What does the ____Bible____ say about sex?

1. Your sexuality is a marvelous ____creation____ of God.

For this cause a man shall leave his father and his mother, and shall cleave to his wife; and they shall become one flesh.
—Genesis 2:24

You may want to ask your son the meaning of this verse.

2. God designed sex within marriage so that ____children____ could come into the world.

3. God designed sex within marriage so that you could experience ____closeness____ with your wife.

4. God designed sex within marriage to bring you a great deal of ____pleasure____.

Memory Verses #4:
1 Corinthians 6:18-20

Flee immorality. Every other sin that a man commits is outside the body, but the immoral man sins against his own body. Or do you not know that your body is a temple of the Holy Spirit who is in you, whom you have from God, and that you are not your own? For you have been bought with a price: therefore glorify God in your body.

When the messag is finished, you can turn off the CD and begin working on the project "Burned Up" and the "Make Up Your Mind" questions.

F. Relating to a young woman.

1. Treat young women with __respect__.

2. Keep your sexual __desires__ under __control__.

Important note! At the end of this message, Dennis will tell you it's time for your project. As indicated in Section One of your Tour Guide, we have included a short exhortation specifically for boys on the subject of masturbation. Continue to play the CD until the end of this message to listen to it.
[CD 3, Track 3]
If you decided you don't want your son to hear this now, stop the CD and move directly to the project "Burned Up."

SESSION THREE PROJECT
"BURNED UP"

OBJECTIVE:

To show your child the need to protect his innocence.

WHAT YOU WILL NEED:

- A box of wooden safety matches
- A glass of water
- Paper grocery bag labeled "Project Three"

PREPARATION:

- Place matchbox and a glass or plastic cup in the "Project Three" bag.
- See page xlviii for project instructions and a script.

The most important thing I learned from this project was:

Allow your preteen time to write comments.

MAKE UP YOUR MIND

If you sense your son needs to talk more, ask him if he has any questions he'd like to discuss about sex or if there's anything he has wondered about.

Part One: Sexual Maturity Questionnaire

What is your biggest question or fear about your body and how you are developing?

How do you think other preteens/teens view your physical and emotional maturity?

What do you think is the purpose of sex?

What does the Bible say about sex?

Before today, what percent of everything you had learned about sex came from the following? (The total should equal 100 percent.)

______ Dad ______ Mom

______ Brothers/sisters ______ School

______ Friends ______ Church

______ Media (TV, Internet, magazines, etc.)

______ Other

Place one of the Adventure Stamps in your child's *Adventure Journal* at the end of Session Three. You should sign and date his page.

With whom would you prefer to talk about sex?

Part Two: Discussion

With your parent, talk about your answers to each of the questions in the Sexual Maturity Questionnaire.

You have completed Session Three of Passport2Purity!

SESSION 4

Staying Pure

Topics:

* How far should I go?
* Establishing boundaries
* Where God draws the line (beyond abstinence)
* How to keep your way pure

Memory Verse:

* Song of Solomon 8:4

Project:

"Leaky Balloon" — is your prep done?

Passport2Purity®

A ______________________

B ______________________

C ______________________

D ______________________

E ______________________

F ______________________

G ______________________

H ______________________

I ______________________

J ______________________

- Lying down while passionately hugging and kissing
- Kissing
- Touching below the neck
- Holding hands
- Touching below the waist
- Being alone with the opposite sex
- Passionate hugging and kissing
- Intercourse
- Hugs
- Taking clothes off

SAFEST

I H G F E D C B A

J

MOST DANGEROUS

splat

Start the CD for Session Four: "Staying Pure." [CD 2/3, Track 4] Dennis will give verbal instructions for what to do with this cliff drawing.

Listen very carefully!

REMINDERS:
1. Prioritize items from safest to most dangerous (pause CD).
2. Restart CD.
3. Put an "X" where most teens draw the line. (pause CD)
4. Your preteen: Draw a line for how far you intend to go (pause CD).

A. Why do you need ___boundaries___?

B. Where does ___God draw the line___?

1. You need to ___trust___ God and His ___Word___.

2. God doesn't say ___no___ to sex. He says ___yes___ to sex according to His ___design___.

3. God wants you to be ___sexually pure___ when you enter into marriage.

Memory Verse #5:
Song of Solomon 8:4 (NIV)

Daughters of Jerusalem, I charge you: Do not arouse or awaken love until it so desires.

C. How do you keep your ___way pure___?

1. By ___thinking___ of the right things (Colossians 3:2)

2. By ___guarding___ your heart (Proverbs 4:23)

3. By not ___looking___ at things you shouldn't (Psalm 101:3a)

4. By ___keeping___ your ___hands___ out of trouble (1 Thessalonians 4:3)

5. By ___keeping___ your ___lips___ off of the opposite sex

Start the CD to continue Session Four: "Staying Pure." [Track 7]

Instruct your preteen to write the memory verse in the box.

LOOK AHEAD

Now flee from youthful lusts and pursue righteousness, faith, love, and peace, with those who call on the Lord from a pure heart.
—2 Timothy 2:22

For this is the will of God, your sanctification; that is, that you abstain from sexual immorality.
—1 Thessalonians 4:3

You may want to ask your preteen the meaning of these verses.

SESSION FOUR PROJECT
"LEAKY BALLOON"

OBJECTIVE:

To show your preteen how seemingly small decisions about boundaries can cause him to lose his innocence.

WHAT YOU WILL NEED:

- A balloon that is strong and large enough so that when you fill it with water and pierce it with a needle it won't burst, but will dribble out a drop or two, and if squeezed, will shoot out a stream of water. We strongly suggest buying helium grade latex balloons from a party store or florist. Buy extras in case one bursts.
- A thin, sharp needle
- Colorful string to thread needle (for safety)
- Water (to fill balloon)
- Roll of transparent tape
- Paper grocery bag labeled "Project Four"

PREPARATION:

- Place all objects in "Project Four" bag.
- See pages l and li for project instructions and a script.

The most important thing I learned from this project was:

Allow your preteen time to write comments.

MAKE UP YOUR MIND

Part One: Questions for You

DECIDE IN ADVANCE: You are at a party, and after a while you notice that a number of your friends are pairing up with someone of the opposite sex. They find isolated corners around the house and begin to kiss and "make out." You've been dancing with someone you've dated a couple of times, and you're asked if you'd like to find a place to be alone together.

What do you do?

Why do you think God wants us to wait until marriage to be physically intimate with someone?

Read and discuss this page together.

After this session, go enjoy your fun time together! Then clean up and get dressed for dinner.

Place one of the Adventure Stamps in your child's *Adventure Journal* at the end of Session Four. You should sign and date his page.

Part Two: Questions for Your Parent!

Can you think of a specific story that illustrates how you related to the opposite sex? Be careful what you share!

What, if anything, do you wish you had done differently to stay farther away from the edge of the cliff?

WARNING! If you got too close to the edge of the cliff yourself, Part Two questions may be difficult. Past failures must not prevent us from calling our children to God's standard. Avoid discussing your failures in this area. Adolescents need role models, not excuses to sin. **Refer to page xxix in your Tour Guide for suggested responses.**

Congratulations!

You have completed Session Four of Passport2Purity!

Topics:

* Dating Questionnaire
* Seeing dating differently
* Your parents need to be involved
* Make up your mind (sharpening conviction)

Memory Verses:

* Philippians 2: 3-4

Project:

"All Glued Up" — is your prep done?

Start the CD for Session Five: "It's a Date!" [CD 4, Track 2]

Pause the CD after Dennis tells your preteen to write his own answers to the Dating Questionnaire.

Instruct your preteen to answer questions 1-4.

Restart the CD when your preteen is finished. [CD 4, Track 3] The audio message will review each question (see next page).

The Dating Questionnaire

1. What is dating?

2. What is the purpose of dating?

3. How old should you be to go on your first date?

4. What kind of person should you date?

A. Revisiting the Dating Questionnaire

1. What is dating?

When a young man and a young lady are alone together.

Instruct your child to write the answers given during the audio message.

Answers from the audio message are provided only in your copy of the *Adventure Journal.*

2. What is the purpose of dating?

To discover the person whom God wants you to marry.

3. How old should you be to go on your first date?

The issue is: How mature do I need to be before I can be trusted to be alone with the opposite sex?

He is also head of the body, the church; and He is the beginning, the firstborn from the dead, so that He Himself will come to have first place in everything.
—Colossians 1:18

4. What kind of person should you date?

a. A person who walks with Jesus Christ
b. A person whose character is approved by your parents

Instruct your preteen to write the memory verse in the box.

B. Seeing Dating Differently

1. Focus on learning how to serve others.

Memory Verses #6: Philippians 2:3-4

Do nothing from selfishness or empty conceit, but with humility of mind regard one another as more important than yourselves; do not merely look out for your own personal interests, but also for the interests of others.

2. You need to wait until later to have a girlfriend.

3. Spend time in group situations.

4. Remember! You are spending time—most likely—with someone else's future spouse.

5. Don't missionary date.

6. Since you're not married, don't act like it.

7. Physical touch is off limits until you're married.

C. Your parents need to be involved in your dating experience.

1. Your parents should determine when you are mature enough to date.

2. Your parents need to be involved in whom you date.

3. You and your parents need to be communicating openly about your relationships.

4. Your parents need to help you set boundaries and guard your sexual purity.

If it looks like your preteen wants to talk about some of these areas, stop the CD and discuss it! This is designed to help the two of you communicate.

D. Make Up Your Mind

1. Will you agree to what your parents say about dating?

2. What boundaries are you going to establish to guard the purity of your heart?

3. Are you willing to wait to truly have a girlfriend or boyfriend?

E. A final thought

After letter E, Dennis will introduce the project "All Glued Up" and end his message. You will complete the project and the "Make Up Your Mind" questions.

SESSION FIVE PROJECT
"ALL GLUED UP"

OBJECTIVE:

To show your preteen one of the dangers of becoming too attached to someone of the opposite sex.

WHAT YOU WILL NEED:

- At least six sheets of construction paper—two different colors (three red and three yellow)
- White school glue (not a glue stick)
- Paper grocery bag labeled "Project Five"

PREPARATION:

- Place all items in the "Project Five" bag.
- See pages liii and liv for project instructions and a script.

The most important thing I learned from this project was:

Allow your preteen time to write comments.

MAKE UP YOUR MIND

Discuss these questions together.

Part One: Questions for You

Will you agree to what your parents say about dating? When? Whom? How you ought to conduct yourself?

What boundaries are you going to establish to guard the purity of your heart? Be specific.

Are you willing to wait to have a girlfriend (exclusive dating)?

Challenge your preteen to consider signing the Wait-to-Date Contract. Do not press him; give him time to make it his own conviction. Ask him to tell you when he is ready. At that time, sign it together. Then place an Adventure Stamp in your child's *Adventure Journal* on the contract.

Part Two: Questions for Your Parent!

Describe some of your own experiences in relating to the opposite sex. What was your experience in junior high, high school, college, after college, etc.? Be careful what you share!

How old were you when you started dating one-on-one? Was it wise?

What one key lesson would you pass on to me about dating?

Part Three: Wait-to-Date Contract

Turn to the next page.

After completing Session Five, you're ready to go out for your celebration dinner. (See page xvii-xviii in this Tour Guide.)

Don't forget: On your way home from dinner, listen to closing comments. [CD 4, Track 4]

You may also want to review the Scripture memory verses that are at the end of CDs Four and Five

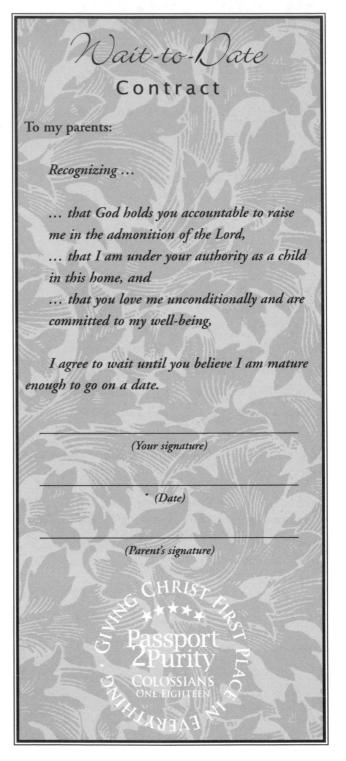

Wait-to-Date
Contract

To my parents:

Recognizing ...

... that God holds you accountable to raise me in the admonition of the Lord,
... that I am under your authority as a child in this home, and
... that you love me unconditionally and are committed to my well-being,

I agree to wait until you believe I am mature enough to go on a date.

____
(Your signature)

____
(Date)

____
(Parent's signature)

GIVING CHRIST FIRST PLACE IN EVERYTHING
★★★★★
Passport 2Purity
COLOSSIANS ONE:EIGHTEEN

Going the Extra Mile

The following three studies are included to allow you to climb higher. Please complete them sometime AFTER YOUR GETAWAY. You may work on your own or together with your mom or dad. Happy climbing!

Topics:

* **Whom do you listen to? (Peer Pressure)**
* **From shepherd to king (Maturity)**
* **Joe's dilemma (Purity)**

WHOM DO YOU LISTEN TO?

Going the Extra Mile on Peer Pressure

Imagine walking into the stereo department of an electronics store with your father. (Hey, while you're at it, imagine he even likes your music!) Someone starts cranking up one stereo after another, and your head pounds harder with every beat … which is usually okay. But you see your dad pick up a new CD (cool!) and he's saying something—you can hardly recognize his voice—he's smiling. But … what is he saying?

ᘓ

Lots of "voices" that influence your thoughts and actions come at you every day. Some are familiar. Some are strange and new. But you still have to decide which voices you will trust to help you make decisions.

The Bible is one voice that is always true and can always be trusted. No matter what's happening around you, you will want to recognize what God's Word has to say about it. Take a few minutes and look up the following passages to familiarize yourself with God's voice.

1. What advice do the following passages have for you?

   - Proverbs 1:7-19
   - Daniel 1:8-9
   - Jeremiah 23:9-14
   - 2 Timothy 3:12-17

2. Now, choose your favorite passage. How is the Lord speaking to you through this passage about a situation you now have in your life?

3. Ask five adults who faithfully follow the Lord to share their favorite Bible verse with you. Ask them why they chose that particular verse.

4. Pray and ask God to help you hear His voice above all others.

FROM SHEPHERD TO KING

Going the Extra Mile on Growing to Sexual Maturity

David was the youngest in the family. His father and his brothers were not very impressed with him. He had the lowly job of tending the family's smelly sheep.

But God knew David's heart and his love for Him. So, God chose David, who was still a young boy, to be Israel's next king, and God sent the prophet Samuel to anoint him—much to his family's surprise!

Years passed, and David became king, just as God had said. He won many victories in battle and brought great wealth to Israel. God Himself had transformed him from a shepherd boy into a victorious king. And everything he had accomplished was not because he did it on his own, but because the mighty hand of God had led him (read 2 Samuel 7*).

Even before the beginning of time, the Lord had special plans for David. And God has special plans for you!

In a few short years, you're going to have an adult body, an adult voice, and adult responsibilities. As all these changes happen, remember that God is working in and through you—bringing you to maturity.

1. Read Psalm 139, a song that King David wrote, and answer the following questions.

   - Verses 1-6: God knows you as no one else ever could or ever will—the good and the bad. Do you need to talk with Him right now about anything you have been thinking, saying, or doing?

   - Verses 11-12: Name some things you are facing right now. How can God guide you in these matters?

   - Verses 23-24: What does it mean to ask God to search you? Have you given Him permission to search you and know your heart? If not, go for it! Then watch for what He reveals to you.

2. Now reread verses 13-16. Did you catch that? God put a lot of thought and care into your design. He created you with a special purpose. Does this change the way you see yourself?

JOE'S DILEMMA

Going the Extra Mile on Staying Pure

Joe had always been open and honest, and generally, he was a good kid—his dad's favorite. He grew up with lots of advantages and dreams of a great future. Joe's dad had always taught him the importance of knowing and obeying God. As he grew, Joe matured in spirit and wanted to obey God in every area of his life. God blessed him in everything he did, and Joe became a handsome, wise young man who kept himself pure.

But a beautiful, influential, married woman became interested in Joe. After a while, her interest turned into pursuit, until finally one day she just wouldn't give up. Joe knew he had to stop her. He rejected her point-blank—he turned and ran out the door. She was enraged! Joe understood that she could seriously damage his future, but he had to do it! God would expect nothing less!

So, he sat in jail with charges against him that could cost him his freedom … or his life.

ꝏ

Turn in your Bible and read Genesis 39.

Joseph didn't get off easy. Fleeing immorality was probably a new concept with Potiphar's wife—she didn't like it! Fleeing immorality is no different today. In a bad situation, the people you turn your back on will probably have a similar reaction.

You will need encouragement from others to help you stay strong in your commitment to purity. Try to think of one or two people who could help you. Now call them! Tell them you want to regularly meet or talk on the phone to help you stay on track with God. You may give *them* the courage they need, too!

The Rest of the Story

1. After some time in prison, Joseph got a chance to get out. Read Genesis 41:12-16, 37-57 to find out what happened to him.

2. Look up the following verses and write the rewards of righteousness and purity:

   - Psalm 1
   - Psalm 15
   - Psalm 34:15-22
   - Proverbs 10
   - Matthew 5:1-16

3. Next time you choose, will it be sin or righteousness?

KNOWING GOD PERSONALLY

A. God loves you and created you to know Him personally.

1. God loves you.

God so loved the world, that He gave His only begotten Son, that whoever believes in Him should not perish, but have eternal life

—John 3:16

2. God wants you to know Him.

Now this is eternal life: that they may know You, the only true God, and Jesus Christ, whom Thou has sent.

—John 17:3

What prevents us from knowing God personally?

B. We are sinful and separated from God, so we cannot know Him personally or experience His love and power.

1. Man is sinful.

All have sinned and fall short of the glory of God.

—Romans 3:23

2. Man is separated.

The wages of sin is death ...

—Romans 6:23a

How can the canyon between God and us be bridged?

C. Jesus Christ is God's **only** provision for man's sin. Through Him alone we can know God personally and experience God's love.

1. God became a man, through the Person of Jesus Christ.

And the angel said to them, "Do not be afraid; for behold I bring you good news of a great joy which shall be for all people; for today in the city of David there has been born for you a Savior, who is Christ the Lord."

—Luke 2:10-11

2. He died in our place.

God demonstrates His own love toward us, in that while we were yet sinners, Christ died for us.

—Romans 5:8

3. He rose from the dead.

Christ died for our sins ... He was buried ... He was raised on the third day according to the Scriptures ... He appeared to Peter, then to the twelve. After that He appeared to more than five hundred ...

—1 Corinthians 15:3-6

4. He is the only way to God.

Jesus said to him, "I am the way, and the truth, and the life; no one comes to the Father, but through Me."

—John 14:6

It is not enough just to know these truths ...

D. We must individually receive Jesus Christ as Savior and Lord; then we can know God personally and experience His love.

1. We must receive Christ.

As many as received Him, to them He gave the right to become children of God, even to those who believe in His name.

—John 1:12

2. We must receive Christ through faith.

By grace you have been saved through faith; and that not of yourselves, it is the gift of God; not as a result of works, that no one should boast.

—Ephesians 2:8-9

3. We receive Christ by personal invitation.

I am the door; if anyone enters through Me, he shall be saved ...

—John 10:9

Self-Directed Life **Christ-Directed Life**

E. You can receive Christ right now by faith through prayer.

A suggested life-changing prayer:

"Lord Jesus, I want to know You. Thank You for dying on the cross for my sins. I open the door of my life and receive You as my Savior and Lord. Thank You for forgiving my sins and giving me eternal life. Take control of the throne of my life. Make me the kind of person You want me to be."

F. What are the results of placing your faith in Jesus Christ? The Bible says:

1. Christ came into your life (Colossians 1:27).

2. Your sins were forgiven (Colossians 1:14).

3. You became a child of God (John 1:12).

4. You received eternal life (John 5:24).

5. You have been given the power to pursue intimacy with God (Romans 5:5).

6. You began the great adventure for which God created you (John 10:10, 2 Corinthians 5:17, and 1 Thessalonians 5:18).

CREDITS

Passport2Purity would not have been possible without the team efforts of committed individuals and suppliers.

Your Hosts: Dennis and Barbara Rainey

Some contents adapted from *Parenting Today's Adolescent* by Dennis and Barbara Rainey, Thomas Nelson, Inc., Publishers.

Message Outlines:
Adapted from the works of Dennis and Barbara Rainey by Dave Boehi and Mark Whitlock. Edited during recording by Dennis and Barbara Rainey.

Parent's Guide by Dave Boehi and Mark Whitlock

1st Project Coordinator: Ben Colter
2nd Project Coordinator: Dave Johnson

Creative Director: Mark Whitlock

Research Assistants: Benjamin Rainey, Betty Rogers

Editorial: Dave Boehi, Ben Colter, Mary Larmoyeux, Fran Taylor, Dale Walters

Graphic Design:
Design: Lee Smith
Layout: Rachel Mercer
Box Copy: Dale Walters
Illustrations: Steve Björkman
Media Buyers: Jeff Lord and John Stokes
Special Thanks: Jenni Smith, Dan Butkowski, Claes Jonasson

Audio Production:
Executive Producer: Mark Whitlock
Recording Director: Bob Lepine
Engineer: Keith Lynch
Post-producer: Curt Morse for Skynet Media, Inc.
Foley: Abby Morse, Josh Morse, Mark Whitlock
Thanks: Christy Bain, Debra Craft, Phil Krause, Mark Ramey, Andy Watson
Special Thanks: Dina Morse
Audio Drama: All scripts written by Mark Whitlock and edited by Bob Lepine

Blastoff
Countdown Announcer: Neal Moore
Bunker Announcer: Curt Morse
Music: "Cliffhanger" by D. Holter (Network Music 198/1)
Some audio from the NASA archives of Apollo 11 in the public domain

Stampede Music: "Okefenokee" by Y. Goren (Network Music 152/3)

Deadly Skies:
Deb: Deborah Rainey
Les: Leslie Basham
Becca: Desirée Barner, Becca Looney
Mom: Rita Looney
Andy: Anonymous
Music: "Gen-X" by J. Owens and R. Winter (Network Music 186/1)
Movie Soundtrack: "Flashback" by J. Sterling (Network Music 177/5)

The Queen's Knights
Queen: Libby Strawn
Storyteller: Bob Lepine
Gawking Female: Leslie Basham
Sir Vincent: Mark Whitlock
Crier: Mark Whitlock
Sir Arnold: Mark Comer
Sir Jared: Keith Lynch
Sir Connor: Roger Brown
Special Thanks: The staff of FamilyLife for great crowd noise
Music: "Amadeus" by Paul Osborne (Match Music Library MAT 134 CD)

Romeo and Juliet 2000
(With deep and sincere apologies to William Shakespeare)
Romeo: Phil Krause
Juliet: Leslie Basham

Lightening Strike
Alan Treebark: Bob Lepine
Justin Keller: Phil Krause

One Word, Two Definitions
Narrator: Josh Harris

Jeff's Music: "Keyhole Party" by B. Donnelly (Network Music 177/6)
Eric's Music: "Song for Megan" by R. Whitlock (Network Music 118/3)

Scripture Memory Songs
Composed, arranged, and produced by Jeff Nelson for HeartService Music, Inc.
Engineered and mastered by Baeho Bobby Shin
Vocal solo for "Your Word" by Marianne Tutalo
Vocal solo for "Daughters of Jerusalem" by Shawn Dady
Vocal solo for "Do Nothing from Selfishness" by Michael Mellett
Vocal solo for "Glorify God" by Chance Scoggins
Vocal solos for "Do Not Be Deceived" by Shane McConnell and Carrie Hodge

We would also like to thank Jonathan Beaver, Jennifer Blunier, Keri Blunier, Diane Case, Danaea Cheuvront, Mike Clowers, Melissa Colter, Aimee Fookes, David Fox, Christine Franklin, Lori Glenn, Brandon Harris, Danny Harris, Davey Hughes, Stephanie Jonasson, David Todd Murray, Todd Murray, Travis Runion, Elizabeth Searcy, Kathy Searcy, and Kaye Whitlock.

All non-foley sound effects, unless otherwise noted, from the Hollywood Edge Premiere Edition, used under contract.

All Network Music and Match Music used by license from Network Music and Killer Tracks, respectively.